The Great Trail Ride

Text and Paintings by

Jack Terry

Harvest House Publishers
EUGENE, OREGON

The Great Trail Ride
Text copyright © 2000 by Jack Terry
Published by Harvest House Publishers
Eugene, Oregon 97402

Library of Congress Cataloging-in-Publication Data

Terry, Jack, 1952-
    The great trail ride / text and paintings by Jack Terry.
        p. cm.
    ISBN 0-7369-0336-4
    1. Cowboys--Religious life. I. Title.

BV4596.C65 T47 2000
242--dc21   00-024332

Artwork designs are reproduced under license from © Arts Uniq'®, Inc., Cookeville,
TN and may not be reproduced without permission. For information regarding art
prints featured in this book, please contact:

        Arts Uniq'
        P.O. Box 3085
        Cookeville, TN 38502
        800-223-5020

Design and production by Koechel Peterson & Associates, Minneapolis, Minnesota

Harvest House Publishers has made every effort to trace the ownership of all poems
and quotes. In the event of a question arising from the use of a poem or quote, we
regret any error made and will be pleased to make the necessary correction in future
editions of this book.

Unless otherwise indicated, Scripture quotations are taken from the Holy Bible, New
International Version®, Copyright © 1973, 1978, 1984 by the International Bible
Society. Used by permission of Zondervan Publishing House. Scripture quotations
marked NASB are from the New American Standard Bible, © 1960, 1962, 1963, 1968,
1971, 1972, 1973, 1975, 1977 by The Lockman Foundation. Used by permission.

Printed in Hong Kong.

01 02 03 04 05 06 07 08 09 / NG / 10 9 8 7 6 5 4 3

Dedication

To my grandparents, Bill and Maggie Mason,
Whose light will shine for generations.

To Mom and Dad,
Whose encouragement has forever been my strength.

To my lovely wife, Mary,
For her faith, support, and love through our years together.

Special Thanks

To my beautiful and talented daughter, Kelly Luse,
Who taught me to process words and edit copy.

To Jane Randolph and Ruth Samsel,
Who gave me the opportunity to stretch my talents.

To Marc Bennett,
Whose professional photography was picture perfect.

To my publishers, Lonnie and Barbara Crouch,
For whom I have the utmost respect.

To Anita Favia,
For her prayers of support and research of the Scriptures.

And especially to the King of Kings and Lord of Lords,
For it is through Him that all things are possible.

Contents

The Great Trail Ride

Life. Why are we here? What are we doing and where are we going? The mystery of our being, the necessity of our actions, the relations of cause and effect, the dependence of all things upon the other, the magnitude of creation itself and our desire to know the answers to these mysteries assures each of us that life has a purpose that everything points to.

The psalmist David wrote, "Thou wilt make known to me the path of life; in Thy presence is fullness of joy; in Thy right hand there are pleasures forever" (Psalm 16:11 NASB). Everyone wants to experience joy and happiness on the trail ride of life. As a cowboy controls the movements of his horse with a bit, the trails of our lives must be guided by this wisdom, "Thy word is a lamp unto my feet and a light to my path" (Psalm 119:105 NASB).

I was initially guided down that path in the saddle with my grandfather on the bay horse we called Old Dan. Granddad was a working cowboy from an early age and rode on some of the last great cattle drives from Texas to the northern railheads. He ingrained in me the code of ethics that the hero known as the "American Cowboy" adhered to. I listened to stories of business transactions completed with only a handshake. I learned of the rewards of a loving family guided by principles of faith, responsibility, honesty, and integrity.

The cowboy knew that life had a purpose, which was directly linked to a relationship with his Maker. It was not something to be discovered from fortune, power, or personal fame. He was put here to be a caretaker of God's creation. A steward of the land, livestock, and people he loved.

In *The Great Trail Ride*, I will share paintings of the American Cowboy from a personal and biblical perspective as we journey down life's trail together.

Saddle up and enjoy the ride.

Life

Whisper Valley Roundup

Lord, I'm just a cowboy
Like my Granddad who's gone away
I'm really not a loner
Folks just look at me that way.

My life is one of pleasure
I love the work I do
I know I'm special in Your eyes
'Cause I'm made in the image of You.

You brought me into this world
Like a newborn calf in the spring
My legs were wobbly and my eyes were bright
And Your voice in my ears did ring.

You grew me up in this land that I love
With family and friends so true
Showed me the greatness of Your creation
From magnificent vistas and views.

With a good, stout horse between my knees
Down many trails I did ride
Some were rocky and many were steep
But You were always right there by my side.

Life

Like the time we were in Whisper Valley
Drivin' longhorns from daybreak till dusk
The cool mornin' breeze blew through the great bluffs
As hawks soared in the clouds up above.

We herded those cows across the great creek
And up the steep hills high and wide
Through grass lush and green and rocks big as trees
And hot sun beatin' down on their hide.

We rested at lunch in the chuck wagon's shade
Ate biscuits and gravy and steak
We caught a few winks and swapped a few tales
Then tracks for the trail we did make.

We rode hard and fast through canyons and rocks
Where some of us stumbled and fell
Then climbed the great mountain where camp was set up
With a campfire and stories to tell.

The full moon was risin' in the night sky above
As I laid in my bedroll on the ground
The stars were so bright, what a glorious sight
The silence was deafening, not a sound.

Save for the whistle of a hawk on the wing
And an occasional coyote yell
I drifted to sleep in a slumber so deep
It seems You had a story to tell.

"I am the Lord, I've been with you all day
I'm the sun and the moon and the stars
I'm the water and grass and the birds in the sky
I love you, My son, 'twas for you that I died.

"Like your Granddad before you, I'm there when you fall
When you stumble while riding life's trail
I'll pick you up and guide you each day
You'll help others with the story you tell."

When the new day had dawned, I remembered my dream
And I thought of the streets paved with gold
Where my loved ones have gone and wait there for me
I reflected on the story God told.

But wait, I'm a cowboy
With lots of work yet to do
The coffee is ready and the cows are awaitin'
And the trail boss is callin' me too.

So for now, Lord, just let me ride on the trails of this life
Till my job on earth here is through
'Cause I'm as close to heaven as I'll ever be
Till I ride that great trail home to You.

Success

Living His Dream

>+I+<+>O+<+>I+<+>I+<+>I+<+>O+<+>I+<

     Like the lead rider in my painting "Living His Dream," my grandfather was a man who knew where he was going and why. He was able to see clearly even through the fog and mist of hardship and suffering. He was a man of strong convictions and he was always optimistic about the future. When I was just a young child, I thought he was the smartest man who had ever lived and wondered how such a successful man could be so gentle and kind. Granddaddy Mason shared his secret with me, and it has been my favorite Bible verse for as long as I can remember: "Do not let this Book of the Law depart from your mouth; meditate on it day and night, so that you may be careful to do everything written in it. Then you will be prosperous and successful" (Joshua 1:8).

     The world today measures success in how much wealth we can acquire. The rich and famous are often placed on pedestals and admired by millions for their accomplishments. I tend to agree with Albert Einstein when he said, "A successful man is he who receives a great deal from his fellowmen, usually incomparably more than corresponds to his service to them. The value of a man, however, should be seen in what he gives and not in what he is able to receive."

*Success is the sum of small efforts—
repeated day in and day out.*

ROBERT COLLIER

True success in life is determined by how well we handle the seemingly "little things" in relation to the things we view as most important. In 1928, just prior to the Great Depression, Granddaddy was prospering in the cattle and sheep business. With five children and another on the way, he decided it was time my grandmother learned how to drive a car. Few women from the surrounding ranches could drive. The men generally went into town and took care of the shopping while the women spent their days taking care of all the family chores. Granddaddy thought the old Model T Ford would be too difficult for Mamaw, so one day he drove home in a new green Chevrolet. It was a fancy, four-door family car that had gear shifts and even windows that rolled up and down. He was especially proud of that because when it rained they would always have to stop and put the curtains up on the Model T. They were now a two-car family.

Mamaw had always been handy with a mule team and wagon, and she took to driving her new car in short order with Granddaddy's instruction. They drove all over the ranch as he patiently told her every move to make until she was ready to solo. It wasn't long before she was driving into town to shop for the family and friends. While few people owned even one car, they had two. The neighbors in the community viewed them as very successful.

I think the greatest success, however, was that a devoted husband realized the value of a wife and mother who had sacrificed everything for years to care for the ones she loved. She had worked the fields, driven the wagons, raised her own poultry and vegetables, made her own soap, washed the clothes by hand, and always had three hot meals on the table that she prepared from her wood stove. He chose to honor her with a new car. That was Granddaddy's way of saying, "You are a very valuable woman and a very successful wife and mother." Proverbs 31:26-29 describes Mamaw well: "She speaks with wisdom, and faithful instruction is on her tongue. She watches over the affairs of her household and does not eat the bread of idleness. Her children arise and call her blessed; her husband also, and he praises her: 'Many women do noble things, but you surpass them all.'"

I have traveled down two different trails in my pursuit of success. One was *my* way. It left me disappointed, dejected, unfulfilled, and alone. I thought it wasn't necessary to follow the guidance of my family; I could make it on my own. With no place left to turn, I decided to try God's trail and discovered His Word is true. Hebrews 6:12 best explains the important heritage my family has left me, "We do not want you to become lazy, but to imitate those who through faith and patience inherit what has been promised."

In your own search for success, I urge you to hear these words: "Blessed is the man who does not walk in the counsel of the wicked or stand in the way of sinners or sit in the seat of mockers. But his delight is on the law of the Lord, and on his law he meditates day and night. He is like a tree planted by streams of water, which yields its fruit in season and whose leaf does not wither. Whatever he does prospers" (Psalm 1:1-3).

*Do what you can, with what you
have, where you are.*

THEODORE ROOSEVELT

Adversity

If It Weren't for Bad Luck

>—I—◇—I—◇—I—◇—I—◇—I—◇—I—<

As a young teenager, my grandfather worked as a cowboy on a cattle drive from the King Ranch in South Texas to the railhead in Abilene, Kansas. It was a long and sometimes difficult journey. The weather was often severe, demanding the cowboy's expert attention at all times.

As the herd approached the vast plains of West Texas, a ferocious thunderstorm roared in the blustering skies above. With less than half the journey completed, the first obstacle of the drive occurred. The cattle became increasingly nervous, spooked by the powerful wind and crackling lightning. The once tightly held herd began to scatter, moving outwardly toward the cowboys. The experienced hands knew the cattle were likely to stampede, and it was their task to keep them calm and in a tight bunch along the trail before them.

As the lead steers nervously approached a grassy hilltop, they startled an immense herd of buffalo that had migrated south in search of sustaining grasslands. Much to the dismay of the cowboys, the cattle caught sight of the buffalo and a stampede was now unavoidable.

*Whether you think you can, or that
you can't, you are usually right.*

HENRY FORD

Lightning exploded above them as the ground thundered below the powerful hoofbeats of the two herds. They ran over three miles that disastrous afternoon. The chuck wagon and supplies were destroyed in the valley below. The remuda of saddle horses was scattered for miles around and some were never recovered.

The storm blew over about sundown, and the trail boss gathered his men around the campfire and made plans for the roundup. The cowboys were exhausted but they chased those cows for more than eight miles before containing the herd. Some galloped off into the darkness to recover the remaining cattle and horses. The men returned at sunrise with all but a few missing strays. Both the cowboys and the cattle were rewarded with a day's rest before returning to the Kansas trail.

Just as Granddad was caught in the perils of the stampede, we too find that life has its stormy and sometimes disastrous side. Storms come in many forms—tornadoes, earthquakes, floods, illnesses, accidents, angry words—and they all cause seemingly irreparable damage to our lives. If God is truly in control of the storms in the skies, He is also in control of the storms in our lives. Moses wrote, "When you are in distress and all these things have come upon you, in the latter days, you will return to the Lord your God and listen to His voice" (Deuteronomy 4:30 NASB).

So often storms of distraction sweep through our lives and blow us completely off the trail of our destination. Just as the cowboy keeps an eye on the weather and an ear to the ground, we too must be attentive to the storms around us and listen to the voice of God. We must realize that the storm is a friendly reminder that we are drifting from the trail the Lord has set before us. Psalm 34:17 says, "The righteous cry out, and the Lord hears them; he delivers them from all their troubles."

No, unfortunately, life is not always easy. Adversity will most definitely come our way. When it does, think of the cowboys like my grandfather and his friends on the trail who thought, "If it weren't for bad luck..." and remember that when the storm is over, there is a place of rest and a voice that will guide you safely back onto the trail. Jesus promised, "Come to me, all you who are weary and burdened, and I will give you rest. Take my yoke upon you and learn from me, for I am gentle and humble in heart and you will find rest for your souls. For my yoke is easy and my burden is light" (Matthew 11:28-30).

Storms make trees have deeper roots.

CLAUDE MCDONALD

Character

There's One in Every Bunch

A few years back I spent a week on one of the oldest and largest ranches in West Texas rounding up cattle during the fall. The first pasture we worked was about 25,000 acres under one fence. The terrain is very mountainous with large rolling plateaus and deep canyons. The ranch foreman instructed us early the first morning that we were to look for and gather about 850 mother cows, many with calves that were scattered throughout the pastures.

This experience was truly stepping back into what life was like a hundred years ago for the American Cowboy. We rode out from the ranch headquarters at first light accompanied by a chuck wagon loaded with provisions for our six-day roundup. The plan was to arrive at our destination about four hours down the trail and set up our camp. I noticed that the other four cowboys kept watching every move I made out of the corner of their eyes, even though they never said a word to me. I realized at that point that they thought of me as a city slicker and intended to have some laughs at my expense. When you're all alone in the middle of thousands of acres with nothing but your saddle, slicker, and bedroll, you feel rather insignificant.

I knew it was time to make a friend. Ramón was in charge of the chuck wagon and preparing all of our meals on an open fire. He had cooked on the ranches of West Texas during roundups for the past sixty-five years and was a master with a Dutch oven and hot coals.

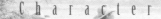

I discovered early on that one of the smartest things I could do was to make good friends with the cook. We were awakened each morning at 4:00 A.M. to the smell of hot coffee, fresh biscuits, and fried bacon. A total of five cowboys slept in bedrolls around the blazing campfire. There was always a race for the coffeepot. The key was to get it while it was fresh as the coffee grounds always filled the bottom. No one wanted to drink the last cup.

Ramón couldn't help but notice that I was eating alone that morning at breakfast, shunned by the other cowboys. He offered me a little advice: "Whatever you do this morning, make sure when you come down the mountain for lunch that you have some cattle with you. You have to prove you can pull your own weight." He went on to explain how the cattle in this part of the country were wild and many of them had never seen a horse, much less a man. He told me they would have a tendency to run the other way and bunch up in the brush.

The foreman sent the five of us in separate directions that morning to begin the roundup. I felt like I didn't have a friend in the world. It's not too hard to get lost on 25,000 acres, especially if you've never been there before. But I took the challenge and rode off as if I were an experienced hand. After about an hour's ride, I heard some cattle over a distant hilltop and began to move in their direction. It seems Ramón's advice was right. The cows saw me before I saw them and ran toward a high plateau. I knew I had my work cut out for me.

I must have run back and forth for miles before I managed to gather one young bull, 18 mothers, and five calves. You can believe I was counting. Ramón's words had made a deep impression. Finally I began to push them down the rocky terrain toward camp. There was always one that didn't want to follow the rest of the herd and was continually breaking out in the opposite direction. On several occasions, big mule deer that were lying in the deep grass would suddenly jump up and spook the whole bunch, forcing me to start from scratch.

A morning alone on horseback in the middle of nowhere allows a lot of time for thought. I began to contemplate the importance of self-control as I was slightly more than agitated at my situation. I could have let the one cow go, but I realized at this point that diligence and self-control must prevail. I was responsible for the cows and intended to do my job to the best of my ability. I was reminded of one of my favorite passages from Scripture, "For this very reason, make every effort to add to your faith goodness; and to goodness, knowledge; and to knowledge, self-control; and to self-control, perseverance; and to perseverance, godliness; and to godliness, brotherly kindness; and to brotherly kindness, love. For if you possess these qualities in increasing measure, they will keep you from being ineffective and unproductive in your knowledge of our Lord Jesus Christ. But if anyone does not have them, he is nearsighted and blind, and has forgotten that he has been cleansed from his past sins" (2 Peter 1:5-9). If ever I needed this passage, it was now.

When I topped the last hill and saw the chuck wagon, I realized I was late for the dinner bell, but I penned all the cattle I had found. I could see from a distance the smile on Ramón's face as he pointed in my direction. I noticed all eyes were on me. When I sauntered over to get lunch, I tried to hide my stiffness from the long ride. To tell the truth, I was hurting from head to toe. I wasn't accustomed to that much riding, especially in mountainous terrain. Fortunately for my ego, the cowboys overlooked my obvious discomfort with congratulations and slaps on the back for a job well done. They offered me a seat by the fire, a full plate of lunch, and lively conversation. I was now one of the boys.

In life, a person's reputation is formed by the opinion of others. It is the foundation on which trust and respect are built. We can't determine what other men think of us, we can only determine what they ought to think about us. Strong character is developed when we are faithful to do the right thing no matter how insignificant and inconsequential it may seem at the time.

Character is higher than intellect. A great soul will be strong to live as well as think.

RALPH WALDO EMERSON

Contentment

End of a Long Day

❯❯❯❯❯❯❯❯❯❯❯❯❯❯❯❯❯❯❯❯❯❯❯❯❯❯❯❯

American cowboys may be the world's foremost experts on contentment. It seems to be an unwritten code they live by. The Maker of the universe has destined them to be caretakers of the land and the livestock. It doesn't matter if the sun is shining, the snow is falling, or the wind is howling, they have a job to do. They always find something positive no matter how inconvenient the situation. Everything seems to work together for the good in the overall scheme of things. Romans 8:28 says, "And we know that in all things God works for the good of all who love him, who have been called according to his purpose." The cowboy knows his calling and his purpose. He never complains about the rain; he knows it is necessary to produce the grass that sustains his livestock. A contented mind is the greatest blessing a person can enjoy in this world.

While rounding up cattle on a large West Texas ranch late one fall afternoon, I watched this scene transpire before my eyes. The sun was setting in the west and the large herd of cattle that had moved on ahead filled the sky with dust, causing a haze over the Davis Mountains in the background. A job that began around the campfire at 4:00 A.M. would soon be complete. As a cowboy riding a white horse sat up tall in his saddle to take in the magnificent view, the last few head of stragglers were pushed into the corral below.

It would be easy to complain about the exploits of the day's cattle drive. We had driven, roped, vaccinated, and branded more than 250 cows. It had been hot and dusty. We had been kicked and stepped on. We had breathed in dust and the smoke of burning cowhide. Now we were tired and hungry, but never once did I hear anyone complain. The apostle Paul wrote, "For I have learned to be content whatever the circumstances. I know what it is to be in need, and I know what it is to have plenty. I have learned the secret of being content in any and every situation, whether well fed or hungry, whether living in plenty or in want. I can do everything through him who gives me strength" (Philippians 4:11-13).

The cowboy knows his purpose in life and is content to gladly do his job, no matter what the circumstances may be. Far from the ranchlands of West Texas, however, discontentment surrounds most of our lives. Our lack of contentment stems from a notion that we have to have the newest, the biggest, and the best of everything. Advertisers attempt to convince everyone that we are either too fat or we are too skinny, or our automobiles aren't classy or sporty enough to convince others of our success. We complain when it rains and when it doesn't. It is usually too hot or too cold. It seems few are content with who they are, what they look like, and what they have.

———◆———

*Do everything without complaining
or arguing.*

The Book of Philippians

———◆———

The primary reason so few find contentment is due to the pursuit of money and self-gratification. The writer of Hebrews says, "Keep your lives free from the love of money and be content with what you have, because God has said, 'never will I leave you; never will I forsake you.' So we say with confidence, 'The Lord is my helper; I will not be afraid. What can man do to me?' Remember your leaders, who spoke the word of God to you. Consider the outcome of their way of life and imitate their faith. Jesus Christ is the same yesterday and today and forever" (Hebrews 13:5-8).

The cowboy has learned to depend on God, trusting that He will supply everything he needs to sustain his way of life. When our goal is the pursuit of material things, we are ignoring God's promise to supply all that we need. We should all learn to be content with what we have, but never be satisfied in our pursuit of excellence in Him.

Happiness is inward, and not outward; and so, it does not depend on what we have, but on what we are.

Henry Van Dyke

Courage

The Riders of Mystic Canyon

Early in my career as an artist, I was invited to the small West Texas border town of Lajitas to do an art exhibit at a local museum. Lajitas was once a trading post that was used for over two hundred years by traders from Spain, Mexico, and Texas. The current owner of the trading post was a colorful character who had many tales and stories passed down from his great-grandfather, the founder of the post. This area has a rich culture and the natives are a very superstitious people.

During my visit I met a young man named Juan. He was from Mexico and had crossed the Rio Grande seeking a prosperous future in America. When he found out I was an artist, he thought I might have some interest in painting what he described as one of the most beautiful places in all of Mexico. Directly south of Lajitas is a vast and often treacherous desert. The small village he called home was some eighty miles away. He eagerly offered to guide me there to photograph the scenery and meet his family.

Early the next morning, Juan's brother met us across the border in his pickup and we began our long and dusty journey. The truck broke down on two occasions, but we managed to enter the small village by noon that hot summer day. We were cordially greeted by his mother. Although she spoke no English, I felt welcomed by her warmth and hospitality and enjoyed a traditional Mexican lunch of stacked enchiladas that she had prepared in my honor.

A man of courage is also full of faith.

CICERO

Juan's brother left after lunch and soon joined us with three horses. We promptly began our journey to the canyon. Juan related many of the superstitions about the mysterious locale as we rode through the Mexican desert. Natives in the area believed it to be haunted. There were century-old tales of people who entered the canyon never to be seen again. It was believed that after the sun had set in the west, various ghosts and apparitions could be heard moving throughout the canyon walls.

When we arrived at our destination, the first thing I saw was a crystal clear stream of water pouring from massive rocks leading into the canyon. I thought this to be most unusual as I had not seen water since we crossed the Rio Grande some eighty miles to our north. I asked Juan if he thought it was safe to ride down into the canyon, admitting some anxiousness on my part. Soon the sun would set, magnifying my apprehension. It was here I remembered a Bible verse about water flowing out from between the rocks. In Psalm 78:15,16, David describes the wanderings of the children of Israel, "He split the rocks in the desert and gave them water as abundant as the seas; he brought streams out of a rocky crag and made water flow down like rivers." I imagined this area to be identical as we entered the canyon between the massive rock bluffs on either side.

The temperature outside the canyon was over 100 degrees, but as soon as we entered, it dropped dramatically. Waterfalls flowed directly from holes in the large crevices above our heads. Fern and other vegetation grew everywhere as though we were in a tropical forest. Not a word was spoken as we slowly guided our horses down the narrow path leading to a fifty-foot waterfall at the back of the canyon.

As the path ended, we were forced to turn a corner. Juan pointed to a rock outcropping where pictographs had been painted by ancient ones hundreds of years ago. As I stopped to examine the images, the wind blew eerily between the canyon walls.

I never thought I was superstitious until I looked at the sky and suddenly became aware of the impending darkness. I was in a foreign country with strangers and no one knew of my whereabouts. The shrill howling of coyotes filled the night air. I was overwhelmed with uncertainty and anxious to return to safety. I was truly elated to see the smile on the face of Juan's mother when we returned home that evening.

*Courage is being scared to death—
and saddling up anyway.*

JOHN WAYNE

There are many occasions in life where we are in unfamiliar situations that require us to have courage. We need to have the mental and moral strength to persevere and withstand danger, fear, and difficulty. We need to hear the words God spoke to Joshua, "Be strong and very courageous. Be careful to obey all the law my servant Moses gave you; do not turn from it to the right or to the left, that you may be successful wherever you go. Do not let this Book of the law depart from your mouth; meditate on it day and night, so that you may be careful to do everything written in it. Then you will be prosperous and successful. Have I not commanded you? Be strong and courageous. Do not be terrified; do not be discouraged, for the Lord your God will be with you everywhere you go" (Joshua 1:7-9).

Family

When Della Rode with Daddy

━━━◆━━◯━━◆━━◇━━◆━━◯━━◆━━

The year was 1929 and my grandparents and other members of the family were living on a ranch near Eden, Texas. Families were generally large in those days, as it took many hands to manage the ranch chores in the most economical manner. This was the first year of the Great Depression, and many people were having a difficult time making their land payments and maintaining their properties. Many people had no place to live and little food to eat. There were five children in the Mason household at that time, plus grandparents and a number of aunts and uncles. My grandfather was an astute rancher and businessman who managed to survive comfortably during these hard times in our nation's past. It was not unusual for him to reach out to assist friends and neighbors who were in financial need.

My mother was born that year, the last of six children. My grandmother, an amazing woman, delivered all her babies at home. No doctor was available at the time, but living in ranch country, they had a veterinarian friend who assisted with the delivery. My mother grew to be the apple of her father's eye. She always loved riding horseback with her dad, tending to various ranch chores. Most of the other children were considerably older and had their own responsibilities around the ranch. She cherished the time she spent with her dad.

Children are a poor man's riches.

ENGLISH PROVERB

My painting "When Della Rode with Daddy" depicts a typical workday during roundup time. My mother was three years old and enjoyed every minute riding Old Dan with her dad. It was that year Granddad bought her a black Shetland pony. Her name was Patsy, and Mother rode her almost every day. She was too young to ride the distance from pasture to pasture, so oftentimes, Granddaddy would take the back seat out of the old Model T Ford, load Patsy in the back, and drive Mother to the next pasture so she could ride out with the cowhands.

It was love and dedication that bound their large family together. Everyone was important and valued, each contributing to the well-being of the others. They understood the importance of working together, taking to heart the passage from Ecclesiastes that says, "Two are better than one, because they have a good return for their work: if one falls down, his friend can help him up. But pity the man who falls and has no one to help him up. Also, if two lie down together they will keep warm. But how can one keep warm alone? Though one may be overpowered, two can defend themselves. A cord of three strands is not quickly broken" (Ecclesiastes 4:9-12).

Granddaddy Mason lived his life by God's principles and passed them down to his family. He always modeled the characteristics of godliness. He exemplified the fruit of the Spirit, which is "love, joy peace, patience, kindness, goodness, faithfulness, gentleness and self control" (Galatians 5:22,23).

The United States was established as one nation under God, yet we as a society have drifted further and further away from the principles that directed our founding fathers and guided our families. Biblical principles are the backbone of our Constitution and have guided families for generations, yet society continues to move away from these values. From the once agriculturally based economy to the Industrial Revolution, and presently into the age of high technology, priorities have changed. Family members who once lived and worked together as a unit are today independent and often separated by many miles, each one pursuing their own goals and aspirations.

Strength of character may be learned at work,
but beauty of character is learned at home.

HENRY DRUMMOND

When we take time to reflect upon lifestyles and priorities of the past century, we must surely notice that we have drifted from the principles that are so important to our families. Perhaps the words of David can steer us back on the right trail: "Unless the Lord builds the house, its builders labor in vain. Unless the Lord watches over the city, the watchmen stand guard in vain. In vain you rise early and stay up late, toiling for food to eat—for he grants sleep to those he loves" (Psalm 127:1, 2).

Faith

Morning on the Merced

❖━┃━◆━◯━◆━┃━◇━┃━◆━◯━◆━┃━❖

      Having been born and raised in Texas, I had never experienced anything like Yosemite National Park in California. As I drove the winding roads leading into the park to meet a friend, I will never forget the impression I had upon viewing the Yosemite Valley for the first time. I was so overwhelmed by the landscape I could not drive any farther. I stopped the car and got out, lost in the magnitude of God's glorious creation. I felt so insignificant in comparison to its grandeur.

      Eventually I continued my journey down the mountain, and was overcome again by the mammoth size of the sequoia trees guarding the entrance into the park. Yosemite National Park includes nearly 1200 square miles of the most breathtaking scenery in the world.

      Upon arriving at my friend's cabin, I was happy to find that he had prepared mountain horses for our journey along various wilderness trails. As eagles soared in the skies above us, we rode to vistas where the view seemed to be an eternity away. The mountain paths took us past roaring waterfalls cascading hundreds of feet down towering walls of shining granite. As we continued past rushing mountain streams and calm jade lakes to an alpine meadow, I was consumed by the presence of the Lord.

The smallest seed of faith is better
than the largest fruit of happiness.

HENRY DAVID THOREAU

I was reminded of the verse in Psalm 46:10, "Be still, and know that I am God; I will be exalted among the nations, I will be exalted in the earth." When we stand quietly before the Lord and honor Him with our reverence and praise Him for His power and majesty, He is faithful to reward us with His presence.

Faith is a precious gift from God. The writer of Hebrews tells us, "Now faith is being sure of what we hope for and certain of what we do not see. This is what ancients were commended for. By faith we understand that the universe was formed at God's command, so that what is seen was not made of what is visible" (Hebrews 11:1). Faith is something that is sure and certain. Faith begins when we believe that God is who He says He is. When we take God at His word and believe His promises, then we demonstrate true faith.

If you want to experience a faith-building relationship with the Creator of the universe, Jesus said, "Ask and it will be given to you; seek and you will find; knock and the door will be opened to you. For everyone who asks receives; he who seeks finds; and to him who knocks, the door will be opened" (Matthew 7:7,8).

*I am one of those who would rather sink
with faith than swim without it.*

STANLEY BALDWIN

Honesty

Misty Trail

><+><+><+><+><+><+><+><

It seems like the cowboy is always contending with some type of adversity in his daily routine. Foggy mornings can be especially difficult when searching for stray cattle. There have been many occasions where I have rounded up cattle and pushed them to the corrals to get a head count, realizing there were still strays left behind in the fog. Sometimes shadows and images hidden by the fog are not at all what they appear to be when you get a closer look. Fog can be very deceiving.

Unfortunately life is often foggy due to deception and dishonesty. Honesty is one of the most valuable qualities anyone can possess. It is the foundation of all that is high in character among mankind. The world is always looking for honest men, men who can be trusted and will fight for the truth without compromise. Men who will look you in the eye and tell you the truth. Men who are not too lazy to work and not too proud to be poor. Men whose word is their bond. We cannot be deceived into thinking we can compromise truth because we have seen so many others prosper in dishonesty with no apparent consequences. Remember the boy who cried wolf?

*A true man of honor feels humbled himself
when he cannot help humbling others.*

ROBERT E. LEE

My grandfather was known throughout Texas as an honest man. Most of his business transactions were closed with a handshake because his word was as good as gold. During the Depression years, the cattle market plummeted. Many Texas ranchers found themselves unable to pay their debts and many banks were forced to foreclose on their property. Granddaddy knew that many of his neighbors were in jeopardy of losing their ranches.

Being the man of character that he was, he reached out with a helping hand. There wasn't much of a market for cattle at the time, but Granddaddy knew that the King Ranch in South Texas was buying cattle for fifty cents a head. He contacted his needy neighbors and arranged to combine their cattle with his and drive them to the King Ranch for sale. He promised prompt payment for their livestock. He had no contracts, attorneys, or promissory notes.

Granddaddy assembled a few friends, gathered all of the cattle, and began the 500-mile journey to the King Ranch. I remember his description of the total destitution of many people along the trail. He ran across families who had lost everything in the Depression and were camping with their children along the roadside. They had very little to eat and their eyes were filled with hopelessness.

The herd arrived intact at the King Ranch several weeks later. The cattle were penned and tallied. Granddaddy was paid fifty cents per animal, a paltry sum by common standards, but a much-needed blessing nevertheless.

His companions on the trail drive shared stories upon their return of how Granddaddy had generously shared money, provisions, and food with many of the poverty-stricken families along the trail. It was told that he was always careful to give away only his share, never compromising the money due his neighbors for their cattle.

When I read Matthew 5:14-16, I think of my grandfather's honest and unwavering character: "You are the light of the world. A city on a hill cannot be hidden. Neither do people light a lamp and put it under a bowl. Instead they put it on its stand, and it gives light to everyone in the house. In the same way, let your light shine before men, that they may see your good deeds and praise your Father in heaven." My Grandfather was a perfect example of what we all should be.

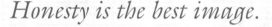

Honesty is the best image.

Tom Wilson

Forgiveness

Pays the Same, Rain or Shine

⋙—⧫—⊙—⧫—⧫—⧫—⊙—⧫—⋘

Everyone makes mistakes. One of the hardest things for most of us is forgiveness. We are quick to blame, judge, and criticize others. But Jesus asks, "Why do you look at the speck of sawdust in your brother's eye and pay no attention to the plank in your own eye? How can you say to your brother, 'let me take the speck out of your eye,' when all the time there is a plank in your own eye? You hypocrite, first take the plank out of your own eye, and then you will see clearly to remove the speck from your brother's eye" (Matthew 7:3-5). This is simple advice, but it seems to be one of the most difficult principles to practice.

The painting "Pays the Same, Rain or Shine" took place on a ranch in Big Bend National Park in Texas. This rainy autumn day was the beginning of the fall cow works. We were riding from the ranch headquarters to a distant pasture to set up camp around the chuck wagon for a week-long stay. One of the most miserable things for a cowboy is a long ride in a wet saddle. Since cowboys never complain about the rain, they knew it was time to don their slickers and mount up when ranch foreman Jim met them that morning at the tack room and said, "Well boys, we pay the same, rain or shine."

A long day it was indeed. The rain fell relentlessly for hours, making for a difficult trip through the mountainous terrain. The ground was muddy and slick—especially for the mules pulling the heavily loaded chuck wagon. They had great difficulty negotiating the steep inclines, often sliding out of control. Upon nearing their destination, it was necessary to descend the mountainous plateau before reaching their campsite in the meadow below.

It is easy to forgive others their mistakes; it takes more grit to forgive them for having witnessed your own.

JESSAMYN WEST

The wagon boss had a tight grip on the reigns as the mules cautiously approached the edge of the plateau and began to make their way down the mountain. He failed to notice the clear path to the right and instead headed directly for the rocks. At that very moment, the weight of the wagon was too much for the mules to control, and it began to slide down the rocky slope. A wheel caught on a large rock outcropping, forcing the wagon onto its side. It threw both men from the wagon, but somehow the mules stayed on their feet. Spooked as they were by the crash, they began to run for the meadow below dragging the wagon behind them. The provisions were scattered all the way down the muddy hillside.

Fortunately no one was injured during this disastrous beginning. After the rain stopped, the men were able to tie their lariats onto the wagon and with the strength of their horses they pulled it upright and gathered the provisions from the mountainside. The camp was finally set up, a fire was built, and the cowboys were able to relax with a cup of coffee.

It would have been very easy for the men to blame the wagon boss for his mistake, but instead all was forgiven. "It could have happened to anybody. Don't worry about it. I'm just glad no one was hurt," said Jim.

Friendships flourish at the fountain of forgiveness.

WILLIAM ARTHUR WARD

Everyone makes mistakes. Some appear to be more serious than others, but in God's eyes, our responsibility is the same. We must forgive everything. Jesus said, "If you forgive men when they sin against you, your heavenly Father will forgive you. But if you do not forgive men their sins, your Father will not forgive your sins" (Matthew 6:14-16). He also goes on to say, "Be merciful, just as your Father is merciful. Do not judge, and you will not be judged. Do not condemn, and you will not be condemned. Forgive, and you will be forgiven" (Luke 6:37).

Love
Crossing the Nueces

The Nueces River is one of the most beautiful sights in Texas. Artesian springs supply crystal clear water that flows for many miles over a limestone rock bottom through the hill country. I had been gathering a herd of longhorn cattle with friends and we found ourselves working much later than we had intended that day. A full moon was rising in the east. What a spectacular sight it was, its white light glistening from the surrounding hills and trees and reflecting from the splashing water under the cattle.

I recall gazing down into the river as I rode across, thinking how muddy and disturbed the usually clear and calm water was. After crossing the river and penning the longhorns, I walked back down to the shoreline and sat on the bank. I was mesmerized by the intensity of the moon illuminating the Lord's creation surrounding me. I gazed into the water, which was now calm and returning to its normal clarity.

Life is oftentimes like that river. Things may appear clear one minute and muddy the next. When we stray from the foundational principles the Lord has set before us, the waters of life become choppy and muddy. But as we return to God's principles of faith, hope, and love, the waters will gradually become clear and calm again.

No love, no friendship can cross the path of our destiny without leaving some mark on it forever.

FRANCOIS MAURIAC

I believe love is the greatest of all human qualities because God is love and His love is the source of our love. The most thorough explanation of love is found in the Bible:

If I have the gift of prophecy and can fathom all mysteries and all knowledge, and if I have a faith that can move mountains, but have not love, I am nothing. If I give all I possess to the poor and surrender my body to the flames, but have not love, I gain nothing. Love is patient, love is kind. It does not envy, it does not boast, it is not proud. It is not rude, it is not self-seeking, it is not easily angered, it keeps no record of wrongs. Love does not delight in evil but rejoices with the truth. It always protects, always trusts, always hopes, always perseveres. Love never fails. But where there are prophecies, they will cease; where there are tongues, they will be stilled; where there is knowledge, it will pass away. For we know in part and we prophesy in part, but when perfection comes, the imperfect disappears. When I was a child, I talked like a child, I thought like a child, I reasoned like a child. When I became a man, I put childish ways behind me. Now we see but a poor reflection as in a mirror; then we shall see face to face. Now I know in part; then I shall know fully, even as I am fully known. And now these three remain; faith, hope and love. But the greatest of these is love (1 Corinthians 13:2-13).

Without love it is impossible to be truly productive or effective in any aspect of life, whether it be our personal relationships, our profession, or our spiritual service. The Bible teaches that love is unconditional and must be directed outward toward others rather than inward toward ourselves. We are instructed to give, expecting nothing in return, and to love others more than we love ourselves. This kind of love contradicts our natural inclinations toward self-centeredness. I am slowly beginning to understand the only way to attain this love for others is to ensure that my faith, which is founded upon God's Word, and my hope, which is a joyful expectation of eternal salvation, are in proper perspective.

It is almost impossible to imagine what this world would be like if we all adhered to the words of the apostle Paul, "Do nothing out of selfish ambition or vain conceit, but in humility consider others better than yourselves" (Philippians 2:3). This is God's plan, and therein lies our map for the trail before us.

If you would be loved, love, and be loveable.

BENJAMIN FRANKLIN

Wisdom
The Last Bunch

>-I-◆-I-◆-O-◆-◆-I-◆-I-◆-I-◆-I-◆-I-◆-O-◆-◆-I-◆-<

When I was three years old, I sat at the knee of my grandmother and watched her paint beautiful landscapes and still lifes. At that early age I had a strong desire to draw and imitate what she was doing. My family realized that I had a special gift and was very encouraging and supportive. As the years passed, I sought instruction and counsel from successful professionals. I knew by the age of twelve that God had a plan for my life.

I've discovered it's critical to seek wisdom in order to discover the plan that God has for our lives. The writer of Proverbs says, "In his heart a man plans his course, but the Lord determines his steps" (Proverbs 16:9).

So many times in life we think we have enough wisdom and don't need any advice from anyone, but it's easy to evaluate our wisdom, or the lack of it, by the way we act and the decisions we make. I have made many wrong decisions in my life and have suffered the consequences. I am certain that had I sought godly wisdom and righteous counsel, most of those wrong decisions could have been avoided.

The book of Proverbs defines wisdom in a few simple verses: "The fear of the Lord is the beginning of wisdom, and knowledge of the Holy One is understanding" (9:10). "The way of a fool seems right to him, but a wise man listens to advice" (12:15). "Plans fail for lack of counsel, but with many advisors they succeed" (15:22).

> *The trail is the thing, not the end of the trail. Travel too fast and you miss all you are traveling for.*
>
> LOUIS L'AMOUR

We all make many decisions in our lives, and it is imperative that we seek God's guidance and wisdom in even the smallest matters. Sometimes His answers come immediately, and sometimes they take much longer. On these occasions it is best to have patience as Abraham did. God said to Abraham, "'I will surely bless you and give you many descendants.' And so after waiting patiently, Abraham received what was promised" (Hebrews 6:14,15). Abraham had to wait 25 years for the fulfillment of the son God had promised him. God *always* keeps His promises. "We have this hope as an anchor for the soul" (Hebrews 6:19). Patience comes through wisdom. When we feel like we have waited an eternity for an answer or direction, the Bible and the counsel of mature Christians encourage us to wait for God and His perfect timing to meet our needs.

In the painting "The Last Bunch" I depict two cowboys who happen to be father and son. They're gathering the last few strays from a pasture in the San Joaquin Mountains of California. Just as my grandfather shared the wisdom necessary for being a successful rancher with his family, this man has taught his son the same valuable lessons. He has passed down the importance of being a good husband and father. He has taught him how to be a good steward of the land and how to care for his livestock. Things one can't learn in school—like stretching a fence straight and true or throwing a rope with precision—are best mastered at the hand of an experienced professional.

Wisdom can be absorbed from the wise like a sponge absorbs water if we are willing to heed the opportunity. God has a plan full of opportunities and He is a rewarder of those who diligently seek Him. Paul wrote, "And we know that in all things God works for the good of those who love him, who have been called according to his purpose" (Romans 8:28).

The wise father of Proverbs said it this way:

> Listen, my sons, to a father's instruction; pay attention and gain understanding. I give you sound learning, so do not forsake my teaching. When I was a boy in my father's house, still tender, and an only child of my mother, he taught me and said, "lay hold of my words with all your heart; keep my commands and you will live. Get wisdom, get understanding; do not forget my words or swerve from them. Do not forsake wisdom, and she will protect you; love her, and she will watch over you. Wisdom is supreme; therefore get wisdom. Though it cost all you have, get understanding. Esteem her, and she will exalt you; embrace her, and she will honor you. She will set a garland of grace on your head and present you with a crown of splendor. Listen, my son, accept what I say, and the years of your life will be many. I guide you in the way of wisdom and lead you along straight paths. When you walk, your steps will not be hampered; when you run, you will not stumble. Hold on to instruction, do not let it go; guard it well, for it is your life (Proverbs 4:1-13).

His wisdom is infinite; that of which
we are ignorant is contained in Him,
as well as the little that we know.

JOHANNES KEPLER

Prayer

The Chase

>—|—◆—O—◆—|—◇—|—◆—O—◆|—<

I did a painting a few years ago called "The Chase." I was driving through New Mexico late one summer afternoon as a rain shower was passing in front of the setting sun. I noticed a lone cowboy in the distance with his rope in the wind in hot pursuit of a wild mustang. Over the next few minutes I watched him throw his rope unsuccessfully as the dust rose above the flowering yellow chamissa blooms. He was determined to catch that horse despite the roar of lightning in the background and the threat of imminent rain. After several tries, he finally captured the mustang and led him across the vast prairie. His persistence paid off.

When I think of prayer and my own prayer life, the image of that persistent cowboy comes to mind. Am I persistent in prayer? I find myself asking that question. Sometimes it seems that God answers our prayers quickly and other times it seems like He may never answer us at all. But Scripture promises, "This is the confidence we have in approaching God: that if we ask anything according to his will, he hears us. And if we know that he hears—whatever we ask—we know that we have what we asked of him" (1 John 5:14,15). The answer to our prayers will either be "yes," "no," or "wait." God has a plan for each of our lives and He answers our prayers according to His will and in His time. Oftentimes it requires persistence on our part as we strive to improve our ability to hear Him. Like the cowboy in "The Chase," we must persist in our prayers through the distractions of life.

*Anything large enough for a wish
to light upon, is large enough to
hang a prayer upon.*

GEORGE MACDONALD

My young friends Bryan and Kristen Winfield have recently experienced the power of persistence in their prayer life. They wanted to have children for a long time but a medical problem convinced their doctors that it would never be possible. But through prayer, they experienced God-given hope and their faith remained strong. They prayed earnestly for five years—both privately and within their church. They sensed God was telling them He was in control of the situation and they should wait patiently.

Kristen conceived the week of Easter and their faith and prayers were rewarded with the birth of a son the week before Christmas, much to the amazement of the doctors. God had answered their prayers with a healthy and handsome baby boy who will perpetuate their family name.

My grandmother prayed for her family's salvation for many years before God answered her prayers. Most of the old-time cowboys were uncomfortable in church and would seldom attend. They were not accustomed to the confinement they felt inside the four walls and were much more comfortable appreciating the Lord's creation on the back of a trusty horse. My granddad was no exception.

Grandmother was faithful and determined. She persisted for several years in her prayers. She attended church regularly and frequented the many revivals that came through the small West Texas ranching communities. God answered her prayers one summer during a revival. She convinced Granddad to go with her one night and, much to his surprise, he found the preacher to be a "real likable fellow." The two of them struck up a friendship, and he was baptized that very week and remained a strong and diligent church member for the remainder of his life. The change in him affected all six children and brought stability and purpose to the family. The power and persistence of the prayers of one woman changed the lives of an entire family forever. She was living proof of James 5:16, "The prayer of a righteous man is powerful and effective."

Over the years I have witnessed many answered prayers. Some have been miraculous physical healings while others have been guidance through difficult times. But hearing that still small voice, that nudge or impression that comes so faithfully from God when I need it the most, is my greatest joy. I would encourage you to "pray continually" (1 Thessalonians 5:17).

If we truly love people, we will desire for them far more than it is within our power to give them, and this will lead us to prayer. Intercession is a way of loving others.

RICHARD FOSTER

Humility
Summer Shadows

———————————————————

I have reflected throughout this book on my granddad's life as a cowboy in West Texas. He was truly a man of honor and humility and remains one of the greatest influences in my life. My painting "Summer Shadows" reminds me of how he used to enjoy leisurely rides through the countryside. When we would ride together, he would talk about nature and explain how perfectly designed God's creation is. He often commented on how insignificant he felt by comparison. It was during these valuable times together that I learned the true meaning of humility.

Granddad took his job as cowboy and cattleman seriously. He understood his responsibility as a steward of the land and livestock. His many years as a cowboy had taught him the necessity of following the natural order God had designed to be successful as a rancher and in life. He was a humble servant who did his best to care for the portion of creation with which he had been entrusted.

This attitude was also reflected in his family life. He was the father of six children and cared for many other family members, including both his and my grandmother's parents in their later years. He often cared for his brother and sister as well. Life proved difficult at times, especially for ranching families who depended on a good economy and favorable weather conditions. Events like the Depression and the "dust bowl" drought devastated many families. I recall asking him when I was a child why he took care of so many people. His simple reply was straight out of Romans 14:12, "Each of us will give an account of himself to God and I want to have a clean slate." Granddad remained a humble servant, always sharing unselfishly with his entire family, paying careful attention to their health and well-being.

Whenever friends and neighbors had a need, Granddad would be the first to lend a helping hand. Many people lost everything they had during the Depression and on many occasions he provided food, clothing, and money to help sustain these families. He was not a wealthy man, just a hardworking, humble servant who discovered that as he helped others, God was always faithful to meet his needs. Jesus said in Luke 6:30,31, "Give to everyone who asks you, and if anyone takes what belongs to you, do not demand it back. Do to others as you would have them do to you." He went on to promise in verse 38, "Give, and it will be given to you. A good measure, pressed down, shaken together and running over, will be poured into your lap. For with the measure you use, it will be measured to you."

Granddad loved to talk of the wonders of God's great creation. The beauty of a sunrise and the birth of a new calf were among his great delights in life. He found pleasure simply sitting in a pasture of deep grass studying a herd of cattle and chewing on a piece of straw. He taught me many things on our rides together, most of which I have not really understood until now. You see, he never said a word about humility. He just lived it.

Humility like darkness reveals the heavenly lights.

HENRY DAVID THOREAU

Granddad has been with the Lord many years now, enjoying the rewards of a faithful servant. But the image of that wonderful man is planted firmly in my mind. That great American cowboy stood tall and proud—his white shirt buttoned at the top, one pant leg draped gracefully over the top of his finely stitched riding boots, and his cattleman Stetson hat cocked slightly to the side. I will never forget the smile he always wore and the good word he had for everyone. A true "gentle" man he was.

It is my privilege to step into his place. My wife and I recently have been blessed with three wonderful grandsons, Hunter, Jordan, and Andrew, and one precious granddaughter, Haley. It is incumbent upon me to share the life of this great man with them and everyone. His humility and fear of the Lord brought him honor and a long life. God's desire is for that to be perpetuated for all generations.

The challenge before each of us is to just "live it" as my granddad did. When we lay aside selfishness and look to the interest of others, we become more like Christ, the perfect example of humility. Our goal in our own lives must be that of a humble servant. I'd like to leave you with these words from the apostle Paul. They are the key to order and honor in our lives. They are our guide on this great trail ride.

Make my joy complete by being like-minded, having the same love, being one in spirit and purpose. Do nothing out of selfish ambition or vain conceit, but in humility consider others better than yourselves. Each of you should look not only to your own interests, but also to the interests of others. Your attitude should be the same as that of Christ Jesus (Philippians 2:2-5).